ESSAY ON MASKS

WOLF EBERHARDT

Crooked Circle Press®
Bailey, CO / 2026

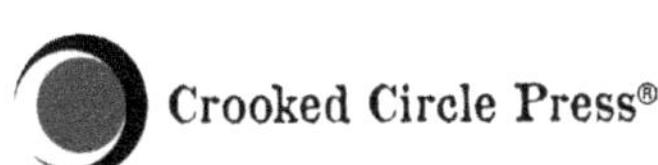

Essay on Masks

Book cover by Jenny Huebner

ISBN: 979-8-9995552-7-4 (Paperback)
ISBN: 979-8-9995552-8-1 (EPUB)

Library of Congress Control Number: 2026936580

First Edition

www.crookedcirclepress.com

For Mnemosyne and the Muses
For The All
And for You

Contents

On Aging

the thing about aging is
it's like a fine liquor
you
become distinguished by the barrel
yet ever closer
to being consumed

Originally published on Medium

Space Heater

space heater
your warmth, i infer red ; tapping those nails on the counter
sitting on my right
you always sit on my right. and i make you smile with mine
when you look (which is pleasantly often, so i smile so you
smile (even though you say "you're bad for me")
and i say "i like the way your new, dark red nails click and make
noise against the counter and against your phone (as you pull
up pictures of things which we had talked about earlier
)even though the clicking was nervous which is why we were
both shaking our legs but eventually we would absolve that)
and i would make myself a fool for that smile

space heater
it's like *Having a Coke with you*
though i am not so privy to all of that art but yours is evident
and lackadaisical because your eyelashes curl up to the ceiling
like they are shy
and also your hand moves on its own when you re apply your
lip gloss which adds the perfect amount of sheen like a still
morning on Lake Wallenpaupack and truly i say and i see that
those eyes are not dark even if you were to look at the closing
of a broadway show
when the curtains reenter and the lights go out and people ap-
plaud; were we there i think they would be applauding the way
your iris shimmers egyptian gold or maybe blood moon
but certainly not black, i have a picture of them in the back
pocket of all my lobes and hippocampus for proof and also the
reflection in my eyes if you'll bite

space heater
one day you may (or so you say
) move away and never look back
and the irony rang vibrant,

for we were walking quickly to the tail-end of twilight (and did you know that that means the light between the two [day and night]?
i did not know that, but it is very pleasant to me and i will surely tell you next time)
it was sort of like violet
Venus begged for attention
"dear if you do go just promise you'll mention or just send a picture of a ghost and i'll catch it" (and i'll wait until judgement day, too—

space heater
why do i call you that for the first time?
this morning i was cold so i plugged in the space heater, turned it all the way up, and had it oscillate and something about that process and the way it warmed the space around me reminded me of you and that made it even more pleasant
unfortunately it is on a timer
probably for safety or self-protection, so it did turn off
and my feet are cold again, but that's okay because i need to go anyway

i do hope this finds you well
- wolf

Originally Published in *The Crooked Circle* on Medium

Revelations in the Playground

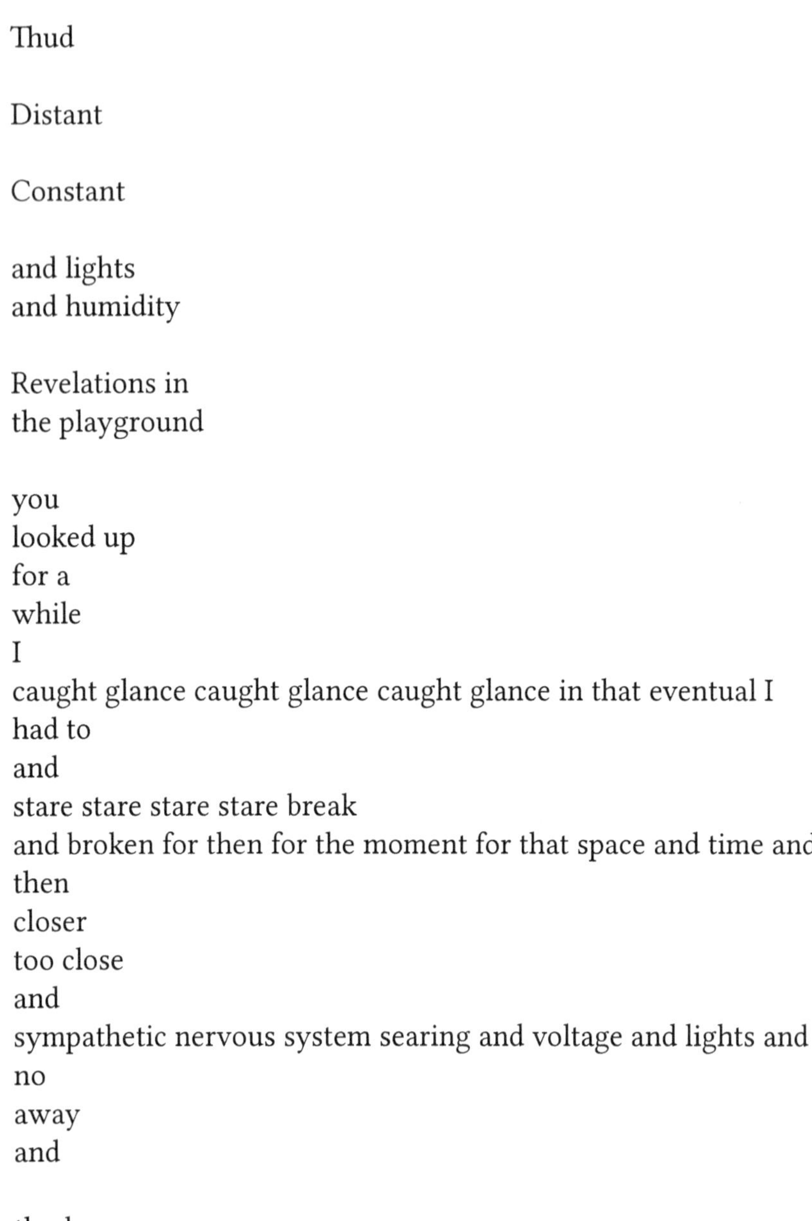

Thud

Distant

Constant

and lights
and humidity

Revelations in
the playground

you
looked up
for a
while
I
caught glance caught glance caught glance in that eventual I
had to
and
stare stare stare stare break
and broken for then for the moment for that space and time and
then
closer
too close
and
sympathetic nervous system searing and voltage and lights and
no
away
and

thuds

again distant and constant and the lights still

the humidity still
Revelations in the playground

Originally published on Medium

Portrait From the Fresh Market Parking Lot

It's art.
Your gait
Your sway
reconciles my
pessimistic circumspection
with its
laziness and
easy thoughtlessness
Quiet confidence.
The effort
of your
jeans and
subtle makeup,
Your hair
glistening as
you walk
lackadaisically into
the gold
of Spring's
afternoon sun.

Originally published on Medium

Popsicle Sky

Popsicle sky, I'm on my way home
Popsicle sky — secret's out.
You melt along.

Popsicle sky, your colors change in a lick of time
Popsicle sky — secret's out.
Your pleasure is mine.

Popsicle sky
You've dripped into dew
A sickle-moon carves
Through Autumn's night blue
Puncture wounds ripping
Star's light shining through
From the outskirts of the infinite.
(to I and to you)

Twilight's death rattle
Swan songs synesthesiacs
New moon black
Oppression, demoniacs
Updated scripture
Well-fed hypochondriacs
Sleep is abuse to
The very rested
(and somewhere a dog is bored).

Popsicle sky, you turn the day
Popsicle sky — secret's out.
We can only stay

For so long.

Originally published in *Write Under the Moon* on Medium

Oak Tree Memory

Do you remember
when I climbed my way
up the

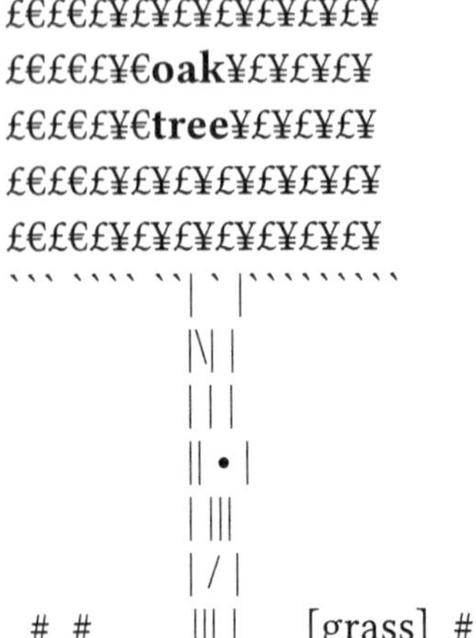

to carve our names into its bark? We got caught
and kicked out of Avalon

And
you almost got yourself
arrested
hot-headed as you are
do you remember that?

Originally published on Medium

Lampshades

If clouds are lampshades for the sun
Then your lips are mourning blue over
A smile that can light up a room
Or cause redness and burning too

We Laugh at Death

We were talking about
Ways to make a funeral unique
and
A video addressing the crowd!
Her: "and don't think I'm not watching you right now!" (laughs)
Me: "and one last thing... (screen goes black)" I looked into her eyes
and it occurred to me in a flash
When I leave this place
I might really be gone for good!
I might never look upon those eyes again. And the wave of Existential Dread
of
Sartre's Nausea
Hit so hard it
Nearly collapsed me into the table

So I drank my beer

What else?

Originally published on Medium

Vermilion

every night i tend to myself by flossing
each tooth and i will
use the pick and
get in there in
some attempt
to mirror
your effortless
smile which has
pulled me out of my
worst days and into that
space that is without pulse or
perfusion as my heart skips a beat again

every morning i tend to myself by putting
product on my hair when it is wet
before rubbing it in and then
i will use a blow dryer to
place it just right as to
mirror how yours
falls so delicately
on your scalp
which
smells of
sweetened vanilla
or what vermilion would
smell like if it did have a smell
and I'd like to tell you about that if
only to see you smile or become shy
since that is to me a heaven on earth

Alone in the Unknown

martini martini
staring staring
out of window at lights on the street
people passing drunk on angst
you looked
so solemn so solemn so solemn
music loud disguising your quiet
blasting the empty chair at your 12
I'd wager you wanted someone to come
up and scoop you right out of your thought

I'd wager you
a few hours earlier
stared at yourself in the mirror
unsatisfied with your acceptance
unsatisfied with
the nervous knot in your stomach
as you saw yourself huddled against the window
drinking a martini alone
waiting for someone to put an end to your boredom
and give purpose to late nights
waiting for the quiet to end
against the engulfing music
to have someone take you by the hand court you down street-
lights
making you finally
not alone
so you broke your own eye contact
moved away from the mirror
and started your car up
and drove
to take your chance on the decisions of a stranger

and so there she sat

at the window alone
and I'd imagined her thoughts
before she stood up
and returned to her shift.

Originally published on Medium

My Sublime

your light
pelted my retina
made a whole scene
thrashed, kicked my
amygdala
on its way back
to the back
to
the back of

   my mind

where it lay I think forever (my sublime
love

Originally published on Medium

Red Sea Parts

fingers wrapped around the curve where your
parietal meets your occipital;
strands of hair push them apart.
a voluptuous red sea—
your lips pouted and open; it was never as wet

as the downpour of waves hugging your temporal
which
ride slowly, melting
down the smooth of your jaw; then climb back up to be pushed,
bent over from behind
your ear

embellished with stones
shimmering high tide's return
with a warm, moist breath in a sigh
as Jophiel sings
I learn your tongue

is smooth, soft
like voices of secrets meeting
in a late dark.
a distant light traces you
I do the same — warm

inside of
you
peek up like the rising of fire
into that space between gazing—ionic it
begins to rain.

Originally published in *Iceberg's Poetry* on Medium

Calypso

The cradle lays upon
white sheets
bronzing her flesh
against them
Her intricate movement
of one leg
toward her abdomen
against the cotton
teases intemporal
with a heavy hip toward the ceiling
hands gliding underneath the pillow
soft
and warm
in the starch
and wrinkles
of an unkempt bed

The room casted
by quiet morning's light
still
as if there were to be
no more mornings
at all

All of the soft plumpness of the room's curvatures condensed at
her
root of it all
Somewhere
leagues and leagues below
Andromeda
Her ocean stirred Amphitrite
Washing away the silence
of a morning not yet intruded upon

by this
or by
that

Originally published in *Iceberg's Poetry* on Medium

The Eroticism of String Lightning Bugs

She said
I don't have to try too hard
I'll do it for you
Okay, miss

[PLAY]

Fleshed effervescence in this dancing light-snow with the
Television flashes and string light glow worms ushered The
drumroll stomach tightenings
and warmest breadth thermodynamics — I can't
breathe

Curtain drop
Oh m

I rubbed my hand over the lighter and painted the
air;~;the music {{{LOUD}}}
(, what a voice)
Sparks → flame → mel
ti
n
g
((
))
((
))

Light-snow sublimated ecstatic butterfly explosions and steam
A wow, lot of it
‼! Chrysalis weak w eak w e ak now
And
A bit awkward
when the flame burnt out

too quickly –

[STOP]

Originally published in *Bouncin' and Behavin' Poems* on Medium

Not This, Not That

Midnight clouds break into storm and song
Rain mars and marries the windows
and melts down over the concrete.
Did you watch
and realize too
That security is found at the limit of danger?
(and so are you

So I hold you close

To what can one attribute mere words
when the wrapping of you in blankets
in a dark room against me
is just so much more?
Felicitous
Serendipitous
They lack your flair

I pull you to face me because I need (to face) you

No amount of darkness can obscure that look in your eyes and
no sound from fans nor rain nor thunder
nor the ruffling hush of blankets
can hide the change in your breathing
No layer of clothing can conceal the movement of your chest
nor the readiness of your body
Where we are is the tension of the gravity of every star
And no words can carry
or hold the capacity for
the small space between our gazing
(And they are not strong enough to hold the weight of decisions
– our silent responsibility

Distance closes in on

Soft
Warm
Wet
Sounds
Caution fades into the blackness standing behind us like omens

I trace your body
And make art out of something I know well
But no word
No language
No literature
Can pontificate the shape of your soul
No artwork from any prodigy
Can find the movement
Nor color
Nor tragedy of your everything
My ______

Originally published in *The Crooked Circle* on Substack

Arcadia

We'll start with "it doesn't really matter all that much"
But we both know it does, that's the truth
There are so many animals
and more people and even more planets maybe
So many galaxies far and wide but we –

It's *still* a lie
and it always was

I can make matter and I can destroy it too
It's all the same.
Except it's not, I was lying.

I'd lost my train of thought
I started with "it doesn't really matter all that much"
But that was a lie like everything else was
And I took you onto my lap in the middle of the siege of Troy
and said
"Hi, Helen"
And I took you onto my body because I am Paris
I took you onto my body like you were merely the Eiffel Tower
And I took you into my heart:
My kingdom of Camelot
Was it warm, Guinevere?
And so I did not lie not
fully
Because when you were there
We were two people on some other planet in another galaxy
and in some story
So I had to lie fully and

Et in Arcadia ego
Even in Arcadia I am there
In the miracle of every world

with a dazzling waterfall of sustenance
around every bend with perennially blooming flowers
Death is still there.

What will we take before it comes to our door?
What did we take?
What will we remember?
(I will remember you, I always have and did when I got here)

Originally published in *The Crooked Circle* on Substack

Lucifer's Wake

I play Lucifer well
on stage
in the garden of ambiguity
I play Lucifer well.
At my birth, 15:13
at the edge of endings
the sun was shining
I needed warmth. I cried for flesh

I am no more me than man is man
I am no more me than man is anything
Art of his own making.
The fading words – son. grandson.
There is not much left to call myself
I am Lucifer
I have you bite the apple because I mustn't be alone

The arid – what do you know of lack?
What do you know of want
and squeezing blood from stone?
The Holiest ran toward isolation
I rip through its vines
and wonder if God turns His back
I play Lucifer well
A torch in my hand
to show and to scorch

And am thus cast away.

Originally published in *The Crooked Circle* on Medium

Chariot

It is crazy to me that
When driving on the highway
Everyone holds death in their hands
And has one foot on his neck.
That at any moment
One could swerve
And hit an oncoming car
With the force of an archangel
Bloodying their chariot
and
Turning carriage and rider
Into one
But no one ever does it.

Originally published on Medium

My Metal Horse

My metal horse has been good to
me
She has surged through
all weather
snow
and
sun
How long can we keep this up?
We used to
take trips together
down to
the Moonlit Beach
(in more trying times)
Just you and
I
That should
be
your
send off
Before I have to put one in your skull.

Originally published on Medium

Old Horses Go Out to Pasture (a eulogy)

Let me tell you about the rivers moving…!
Moving
Move… they move
Like snakes ~~~,
Oh yes, like snakes they're moving
sssssssslllowlyyyyy

Down the open field!…

Slowly now…!

Keep it going…..

Used to ride in an '02 Avalon
Caravanning my ghosts around
………
………(slowly)
………
Used to ride in an '02 Avalon
Caravanning my ghosts around
Down the 135 and Southern State
One hundred thirty miles
To the thousandth
I was young and I was hanging on Is
that why you
Is that why you
withheld all your affections..? I was growing up

slowly.

Real slow like, honey

Something happened to the chariot's soul
?Computer?Transmission?

Nobody knows
Or knew
So I pushed her out to pasture
By the soles of my shoes
It was
Into the black and
Out of the blue

(And I got me 500 dollars for her)
Snakes risen from Earth,
Lowborns:
Post your ruse
Blend in where you can
And don't you go displaying a clue
Like a check engine light and no codes
Honey, it started moving
S
 s
s
 slowly

(and I Jerry-rigged it so that I could use Bluetooth
Through an FM transmitter, or something like that
Waiting for pairing...)

And that was half of the battle
Brakes molasses, fabric tattered
I should have driven her backwards
I should have
I should have
I should have parked her in the ocean on those solo
midnight escapes from the world in more trying times

She got the job done
But emissions failures seem to tend to ruin the fun Or

the dream...
Good things can't last forever so it does seem To
me
To you?

They probably crushed your body
into a cube
After scrapping your soul
Bringing Past to the world
That we drove through together
In those times and all weather
Like on *My Metal Horse*
I meditated your corpse and said:
"Before I have to put one" into your head I guess we've
reached that destination

Rest in peace, old friend.

Originally published in *The Crooked Circle* on Medium

How I Learned to Change a Tire

I told her in my head before it actually vibrated vocal
cords
(and I'm glad that the back of my teeth filtered it) "why
don't they just make the roads out of concrete?"

Gosh, how silly!

How amateurish a thought!

How wrong I was! (and this I realized,,, forgive me
For I think the curve up and out of town to scoop onto the LIE
was indeed concrete and penance enough

The jostling of the universe is far too much!

There was this little individual nuance on the entrance ramp
A very special

Pothole

This pothole was a philosopher!

Very heady!

Likely the greatest since Aristotle
Himself as raw and rugged as the symposiums in
Greek forests
Back when the oracles sat on mountaintops dressed like ashen
snowfall and so on and so on

Yes, up there!
This pothole
united Kantian ethics with Hume's thoughts on the moral
matters which were tinged with wine-breath It united Hegelian

dialectics and post-modern deconstruction of all things stolid,
sacred, and other things and so forth
It used the latest neuroscience on the market to say "Hey, Des-
cartes,
I don't think I am"
(and that last one really shook the world.)

This pothole claimed to know if the Knight's Templar was really
worshiping Baphomet
Or if it was false breaths distinguished by torture and a lack of
pilgrims to guard
And it had an idea of where their naval fleet went (it claimed
Hyperborea
(or a hole at the poles
(One of those things, for sure

Yes, the pothole was very deep

Now I'm reading the morning the next one and I
scratch my head
Wondering if it was all a part of a most devious plan To flatten
my tire!
The very tire
Which has conquered many a pothole
with the Godspeed and force of Khalid ibn al-Walid! I toiled
over coffee spilling over my hasting steps spilling over the
back-and
forth

My left brain said to the right one:
"my good sir, the most cortextual among us are not so privy to
violence.
That evolutionary ectomorphic sort of theory of brain over
brawn
would keep its hands clean"

the coffee is nearly empty in my cup at this point
Right brain: "I learned how to change a tire." The remaining coffee fell down the drain's hole.

Originally published in *Iceberg's Poetry* on Medium

As a kid

Our friend's parents kept a bowl outside for use as an ashtray
And as kids
We'd share a big bowl of popcorn with no
Worry of choking and I'd climb the tree as
High as I could while on rainy
Days the cigarette bowl looked like a yellow lake
Opaque with
Singed white logs

And as a kid I remember a time I
unholstered my nerf
gun and aimed it lackadaisically at the
spider on the ceiling and popped
a shot and hit it square in the
thorax so I'm sorry
spider for snuffing you out like
that then I learned about Jainism
eventually and I try my best to not
kill insects or arachnids anymore but it
was a good shot

Back at the Bar

Back at the bar our desperate attempt our lowly
mistress our moonlit respite

Ice in barren cup and smell of old wheat and Sticky sticky
sticky wood and floor
Corner gaze hello
Mirror gaze hello
Walk to bathroom hello
Mirror me that's you gazing?

Venerate that stool, we'd be dumb to give it up There are sharks
in this sticky floor water
They all just got off of their indentured servitude and are looking to numb their mortality

I ignore these things

But sometimes they flush me at night when I worry
"what if I don't wake up?"
Then what was it worth and what is it to be?
…
So back at the bar our desperate attempt our lowly mistress our
moonlit respite!

Originally published on Medium

Remi is Giving Krishna a Run for His Money

So I was sitting outside with the dog trying to read the
Bhagavad Gita for the
first time
Okay, it's going well –
Arjuna is weeping and refusing to fight the evil army Krishna
smiles at this and starts waxing poetic all over him
Like how Being cannot **not** exist
How living is manifest and how
the space between death and rebirth is unmanifest and I really
like that word that Krishna used – *unmanifest*
so you could say I was enjoying it
Then the dog starts barking at me because he wants to play
Now,
I've been sick the past couple days, not really feeling my best
but okay
I pay Remi his dues and throw around his basketball a bit
as best as I could because
well, you know
I'm sick
But he's having one hell of a time
and he runs after that damn thing like
a police dog running down an armed man Enough was enough
eventually and I sat back down It was sunny yesterday and
good to get some fresh air So now I'm back at it and Krishna is
really giving Arjuna the works
talking about how the wise man basically feels nothing and
well I'm not so sure about that my Lord,
isn't that
depression?
And how some are built for action and others
contemplation
Well okay that makes sense
thanks for crediting my stillness,
my Lord

My Lord, he is barking again
and
My Lord I can't feel *nothing* because he won't stop and I don't want the neighbors to
get pissed off
I look to the left and say with as much authority as I could muster:
"Remi, not right now!"
That only riles him up more
So I'm getting annoyed and stand up quickly which I felt in my head
because, remember, I'm sick
and he's a smart dog, he sees the body language so when I start walking over
he rolls on his back, submitting
and I'm trying to look stern
tough as a walnut
trying not to smirk or anything like that
but he's looking at me with the goofiest eyes, mouth
parted open
I had to look away
I got my point across so I go to pet him
I just have to fake it sometimes, see?
Someone needs to show some authority
and if it were him
The house would be up in flames
He'd certainly be a Caligula
a real Hideki Tojo, if you will
Okay, so I go to pet him
and
He springs up and grabs the ball...
Goddamn
The bastard got me.
I know when I've been got, and I've ought to respect the hustle
so I
throw the old, weathered basketball

a bit more
and I'm glad to see him happy Even if that makes him, by Lord Krishna's standards,
unwise.

Originally published on Medium

Kharadama

It's a throggy kind of day.
The evertrees pander a splash of bouts;
the thrashing pellets wetten.
O! The evertrees bow, bob, and weev
twinkling your then did eyes when you sweared on seeing heaven.
(and do sometimes now when I balance the light perfectly)

Oh! Great sky:sunlesssky;skywithoutsmile
What are we to do with you?
The lips are tighter and I fan my scribbled face of your sweat.
Squally little devil!
You make me... Disheveled! Blushethed!
Marooned and subdooned
Sweveled!
I push back up my wettened hairs
The funny rocks flash their gaze on me, sparkling too quick to make acquaintance and they wink your bath and become like my skin in the waves.
The little tortures that do smoothen and smahthen in their must
The little tortures –
can't help but to make wonder you if God feeleth not our pain or so
And if God doeth feel our pain, is it all of our pain?
Do you think therefore you am?
Do you put your best foot forward into a puddle?
Do you do it without rain boots?
Oh pish, the world ina raindrop and all of its fairytales daroom on my face and fall eventually somewhere or go back up to the big sky and do it again and again like Dharma and Karma had a baby and called it:

Kharadama

I wonder if we're the same or not as that little baby, and if that's something that I would wrath against deeping my feet into, for I do not own rain boots.
Maybe rain makes you remember
And at the end of the day we're quite tired of it and that's why we sleep.

Originally published in *Iceberg's Poetry* on Medium

Growing Old

Getting old the atrophy in the light of a new day
Pulled from youth the atrophy in the light of a new day
Glasses on my mantle
The open space, the terrace
Be mine again today
Even in the rain
Even in the soothing sound of Summer's approach
Even as the bell rings and the numbers soar
Be mine again today

Growing old the atrophy the light of a new day
Cruel is nature
Cruel is a system
Cruel is the 3 am moonlight glistening
On her face
Soaring
Down the 135

Becoming older
the atrophy
the light on a new day
Our signals into space
Will live on forever
Our heroes
Our villains
Our well-tuned atomic clocks
Our footprint on the souls in our gravity
Will live in their life
As we atrophy
Together

Originally published on Medium

I Will Always Love You

I will (my
always love
you
(my little gone friend)
I will (carry you
forever
when far feels the end
for too soon was yours
I've tried to make sense
I dissonate thinking of your here as a means

I will (I promise to
carry you
(I already do)
you feel so much lighter
lighter
than you did just last week

It feels so much emptier
quieter
hollower
than it did just last week
than it did just last week
when we played out in the yard
just the last
time

Visage of Connecticut Across the Sound

What a triumph. On the closing of a
Sun-kissed Autumn day, fleshed thing of dreams
The way I dodged the swallowing of late night and the emptiness that trails

collecting dirt. Brown leaves carpet a solitary path
Their weakness crushes what remains
They come apart under my boot

I'd found a fine spot to get it done
A cliff's edge. Overlooking the Sound
It is destined to be by the ocean, it is destined

A match met in secrets.
Tight-lipped puppet children
See me rip the strings? I am weary. You learn by observation

Room for emptiness in another's stomach
A mother's stomach.
Slow death, she is not eating

Burning lungs give taste to distance
More, more.
They say space is expanding faster than light

Do you see me? The way I restrict my smile
One side, the right, rises higher than the other
Lips push on my teeth. They are not mine

Do you see you? Full-faced like a harvest moon
Free from wind, water, and soil
Young enough to still believe in immortality. It is not yours

Mother gives birth to the slow drip

Project onto a field lily. Cross what you can
Winter always comes; the sun dims

A new savior to attinge your scars
Plead with prayers before the tar turns their face
Make them obsessed with the bandage. Change pro re nata

At the feet — feathers spread out and flattened
Evidence of massacre.
Bluebird, where have you gone?

A fine spot to get it done.
Alone as the visage of Connecticut
across the Sound. Silence fills what's left

Originally published in *The Crooked Circle* on Medium

Box Cats

But I think it's nice to get a Rorschach entourage emission plastered onto the occipital lobe
Boxes are nice and just because you're in one doesn't mean you're of one, dig?
Anyone who tries to not be sedimentary will end up pretending to be metamorphic or igneous
Make sense?
They can't be another type of rockstar because all of the tickets were sold
You get it, man?
Ha, and I thought I was talking to myself In a way it's imperative
to categoricalize and then
recognize,
tribalize and organize
substantiized forms of matter
And once you call a cat a cat then you can say if it's Siamese, you feel me?
I feel me
But I'm just a cat
A cool cat?
Heh,
maybe, dog
Some things are not so obvious
and are up to the experiencer of the
experienced
Which is their experience
And there's no other experience,
really
But we do all experience
So, yes
there is
collective experience
Do tell, dog

are *you* experienced?
Ha, I bet you are
little box cat.

Originally published in *Iceberg's Poetry* on Medium

Gray Brain

Inside my brain there is gray.
I have died more times than Christ; you think
I think
Just like Kurt Cobain –
Waddling end of the line, I think
Dsigoranizde; cannot you think?
While my body is serpentine
Phrenology had had its day
Neuroscience shows that I'm lying; I'm wrong
Mother vinegar dormant supine; you know
Apparatuses get weaker with time

Inside of my brain there is gray
Science has ruled out the mind, I know
Can I have just one more drink?
Can I turn off and confine?
I can't be what the army tells me to be
But I could make knots without twine (and I will)
Inside my brain: is it gray?; I don't know
I've never seen it with my own eyes (and I won't)
Empiricists put me to sleep, you know
But they're right about the sunrise; we'll see

Originally published in *The Crooked Circle* on Medium

Return to Sender

I find it interesting that
we come into the world
naked and warm
reaching for mother
draped in white light and white noise
and then leave it
well dressed and perfumed
drunk on chemical cocktail
with hands locked at our belly
in dark silence.

Originally published on Medium

Splatterpatch Portrait

thirsty pot
underneath the leaky
 ceiling
. (drip drop, drip drop
 drip drop
oh,
   no
there's a
        hole

    in the bucket
..

Originally published in *Iceberg's Poetry* on Medium

Flat Soda!

[can]—– -~—– --string~—– -~—– -~—– -[can]
swoda, kinda sawta
sawda?
pop?
CRACK, pssssss
gl gl gl gl gl
kling
[can]–you hear the bubbles dying?~——–[can] narc,
is
us
no good?
your bubbles
mmm, perfect
[can]–you feel it stealing your heat?~—– [can] sister, soldier,
you
Bunzō Minagawa
"Seppuku for
you", you
take, take, take
[can]–you taste happiness on dirt?~—– -[can] Soda spilled
"you, you..!
get down clean my
mess
lick floor,
dummy"
[can] –you remember the—~—– -~——-~[can] Summer day kids
we used to
drink it
with crushed ice
and a spoon
I haven't in years, but
[can]–you? still love?~——-~———— ——- - - - -

Originally published in *Icberg's Poetry* on Medium

Letter to a Friend

I washed the pen before I started writing this It
was sticky
Why?
Well I've been parsing through the
brush-necks
and honeycombs to find out
I could think of a few hypotheses – two, really
But,
my knowledge of Aristotle is toddlerile
So let's stick to the essence over substance here,
And wax poetic, little bumblebee ~

What can I share about with you today
, friend?
Would you like to know how the minutes before departure are?
How they're slippery
Like a bull's tail
in olive oil?
Or how a tired one
snuggles more readily with death?

Here, listen:
The in-between is any old bread
and it's fine at first
You could toast it, make a sandwich...
Agh!
It all goes stale eventually, unfortunately
At least that is the case for me, darling friend
That is okay –I will be making french toast in the morning

Here's an update for you:
I've continued my reading of *For Whom the Bell Tolls*
I guess I'm about ¾ of the way through (then add eggs (There
was no need for that, really. I just like to see you smile))

It's good!
And I'm afraid that's all I've to say
The contrary is over-written, over-produced, over embellished, and....
needs a benzodiazepine
(and I like to make you laugh, too)
I do hope this finds you well, bumblebee. And that it made sense.

Yours Always,
The Flower

Originally published in *Icberg's Poetry* on Medium

A Seed's Story

There in Moon's gravity
come the ballistic tailed missiles
to poke and prod at the lunar module
dead on arrival
a tribunal of stars
astronomers peek
an earthlit graveyard
one hero submerges
to be and succeed
in the binding of
A, T, C, and guanine

270 suns sprinkled the craft
before those hydraulic doors forced their way open
out came the moonborn
quite odd looking thing
recycled, delightful
glory of Spring

Houston cheered and cried and brought it to Terra
gave it milk, no honey
some blue sky
and debt
death
taxes
an accountant
a pet
things to cherish
and others to lose
adolescent angst
and mind-rotting news
Time tells its home
"move further away"
with each revolution

more into the gray

Taken either by
light or dark
taken perhaps by both
light and dark

Originally published in *Bouncin' and Behavin' Poems* on Medium

Pick My/elin Mind

Strum(s my/elin she)ath
(my elin strum sheathes (pick pluck
she eath (er)/um
my line strums pluck my (line) she
ath pick pluck
pluck my |ether|; pick my
m(ind)yelin.
strum in sheats in my (elin) mind
pl.y m y.uck (ether
st ick y u (ck) r she line s n my
mind pluck my/elin

Originally published in *Iceberg's Poetry* on Medium

Of Cedar, Sound, & Age

Of my grandfather's light-gone eyes
The blue that pierced in past had little left to see sky Skin of hand already thin thinning
Held onto memories of Ma's face hold with grinning

It was always warm there
So the calendar salesman whispered of no New Year's sales
A pity
The sun crept through shades
And I listened to the exposed floor's crackle

Now sat I and he at noon-time about
At circular table of blood redoubt
In quiet was noticed the clock-tick for heart's orchestra A most languid choreography and betrayal of Portia Then heard we the chorus of long-buried dryad From clamorous cabinets, a cracking of eyelid Where out came the ancient caturaṅga board Which shook through the air like feather's fall It looked clear to me that an angel hand guide The wizened hands of old baby blue eyes
Who heard the song and placed cedar wood pieces As actuated by his twenties him vigor

---

Originally published on Medium

Imploded Tin Can

Hook me With your **Smile, pleasantly**
up to something and **no one see us**
an ethanol wink I'm **falling.**
I V. confused. You. **but I,**
then hook bait for **weird fish**
me up high. feelings **don't last**
to a drop quickly. **in your ocean;**
writing machine. lows keep **coming and going.**
string up me, slender. **love, is it?**
my fingers Food for **a construct**?
so you must. see. lust? **in your eyes.**
can see. I'm losing **myself too.**
then oogle myself in **and out**
and oggle petty fantasies **there**
"**make pretty** of what **you wonder:**
words,. will certainly. **what happened**?
flunky." never be.**an imploded tin can.**

Originally published in *Iceberg's Poetry* on Medium

Essay on Masks

A mask:
What is a mask?
What is
a mask?
Wutiszahmaszgk (is that a mask?

What the hell
is a mask?
Why can't I write?

Why I cannot write:
I cannot
because
my fingers are (cold
but they aren't
they are perfectly) warm

Oh, and what is a mask, anyways? Eleven definitions, my dear.
Isn't that (ironic
ally fitting
because it's
)funny

(a mask?):

 what is it?, now
my fingers are cold.

Originally published in *Iceberg's Poetry* on Medium

Without Worry

the children are all about on their bikes
pedaling through the rain not a car
the water cannot weigh down not a worry and
at home is a change of clothes and dinner

The Snake Cures Its Kill

The strategist hesitates clockwork
The liar makes eye smile gleam
The kind one says “yes” in defiance of heart The
mother culls action with scream

The open-brained dances on decision
The lender offers sunshine relief
The dog guards its dead-bodied angel
The frost kills the strongest of Spring

The creative exalts their made demons The
jailer gifts meal, warmth, and home The
clergyman kills his no-family
The lover might lose grip to grow

The good is so trailed by its shadow
The bad can elude as the good
The good may do things that make wither The
good must do bad in their should

Originally published on Medium

Sketch of a Left-Handed Vagrant Who Would Make a Fine Fisherman

You donate money to a charity that saves killer whales because you want to believe in something
You subscribe to Time Magazine and put the newest edition in a basket in the first floor bathroom for guests that don't arrive
You walk by the harbor in the early afternoon and think you'd make a fine fisherman
You "hit me" on a 16 because the game is rigged and heroes usually die on their feet
You poise as a frontman for an art exhibit and wear sunglasses at a revolving door
You check eye corners for genuine smiles and cheekbones for austerity
You take out the garbage with haste when it's late so something out of the sky doesn't get you
You make a loaf of sourdough bread but use too much acetic acid
You lose your mind and then you loose your lips when you make too much acquaintance with the walls
You dive into a shallow barrel of dark water and plan against reemerging
You read Dostoevsky to oxidize a formidable ego and it backfires
You flick cigar embers over your pajama pants and see what happens if you don't look down
You park at the tail end of parking lots for peace of mind
You go to the mask store for readjustment by the same vendor every other weekend
You chew on dynamite and remark on how bitter it tastes in your mouth
Your other title is 'About Me' but the mirror is still smudged with yesterdays
You jump in front of bullets that were fired in another town
You build a house of cards with glue and project yourself onto it

You find that you either spend all night bobbing for apples or you can't do it at all
You elect against speaking evil of others to avoid introjects that will crash the car you planned to crash yourself
You buy an ant farm as a celebration and leave it in the backseat of that car in late summer
You play horseshoes with two right hands even though you're a lefty
You build a dazzling castle and then you build a moat around it
You throw old tennis balls at the ceiling and don't like when they come down so you throw them up again
You dip your toes in when no one's looking and wonder what it takes to walk on water.

Originally published in *Iceberg's Poetry* on Medium

Ophelia Lounge

Wide eyes high above the East River
turning
slowly

Dilating in checkerboard floor and art deco
era
lush

Plush red seats, scented mezcal
Manhattan blue June air through the
open
balcony

Little lights move below
Illuminating box prisms of
concrete
earth

In them— little bodies moving
eating dinner to a
glittering
screen

Thick pane cutting out the ambiancing buzz And
over-excited cabmen
dingy
yellow

Golden cell real estate charmer
few floors
below
Eating dinner as the world goes by
What ails
you?

Separate by the odd peace between us
I turn away to look over the East River
"Coca Cola" rings Long Island City to
Beefeater
and bitters

Originally published on Medium

Memoriam

In the reflection of the car windows which they stood in front of,
under the late afternoon sun,
I saw four crinkled eyes, two smiles,
And enough tension to break their worlds

Sunday's Broken Eggs

Ding dong clock rings 11 on day when
Rough cotton suits would fill the station wagon
Then eat bread between bows and handshakes
(oh my!)

Ding dong clock rings 11 on comedown street The coffee's hot as ever so line line line
whisper)Pitter pattering roughnecks for your seated window show
(oh my!)

Ding dong that man's stuck between 1two walls1
Dr. Past and Mr. Present cursing over Ms. Future(ohdoesn'tshe-lookstunning
He checked his dirtadidas and nonefromfamily phone
(oh my!)

Ding dong he's peeking his overshoulders where noone'sfound in nowhere'stown
Bellmore! Bell-more! Bell more! dingdingdingding
Ding dong that egg cracked and walked into the bar
(ohmy)

Originally published on Medium

I'm a Man, Arizona

I could walk down the street at night on my own
I could get angry at the airport when checking my bag
I could ask the waitress for salt on the rim
I could drive for miles and end up nowhere

(my mom doesn't love me)

I'm more lost potential than that to be had
I could love a woman for time that is endless
I've gone on to go on to have hair on my face
My stomach churned staring into the depths

My stomach churned, I thought about falling

Originally published on Medium

Three Devils

Returns from Hell are warranted.

It's late night and early morning, both of them.

Devils scour the tunnel in the dark.

Green

The kid
15, 16? Weak. Not yet gruffed by the days-in days-outs
The kid sits on the curb at the 7-Eleven with his head in his hands
looking distraught
maybe drunk
maybe something else

You – You're emboldened by your facade of wiserelder
You – think to ask "yo, you good?" — wise medicine man)
You don't.

Leave him on the curb to find his way

Red
Work is going well for you what do you do? eyes blazing
I'm an RN give a short smile look down and pay
Oh yes keep working so you could get your alcohol and nicotine!
alcohol and nicotine!
alcohol and nicotine!
eyes blazing he's surely mad

I – give a short laugh

Haha, how's work going for you
silence

silence and nothing just big crazy eyes like marbles in a cursed hall

Leave
Green devil is getting in some car. You missed your chance to play Messiah.
It wasn't meant for me I say in my head not fully consciously but more the idea

Put the car into first and play music but don't hear it
Then bring the windows down but don't recognize the wind either
People on the road so late and so early, they surely must be mad

Get back
Sit in the car for a short while. windows down ignition off
No music, no wind. The pressure in the air is a dust devil enveloping the West
Bird sounds. Expected
Footsteps out of view. Third time and twice in two days. Not expected
and something surely not right like a crooked smile from a corvid
I stare at the fenced perimeter in the deep dark between night and day with no fear like I cast out Wendigos for sport

silence

silence

Nothing happened

I say I'm not mad: I'm not mad

I go inside

I think about *Blue*
Showing up as he pleases
I shoo him away

silence

silence

Originally published in *Wolf Eberhardt* on Substack

Then Chaos, then Later, then Gone

Mom was born with half of you already there
Waiting patiently
To be thrown from the nest
By oxytocin and latex gloves

They say that my time and my fortune
Are in my hands
so
I stare and play at the lines
As it flows on by
Blissful in misoverstanding
Like the Iron Man from Tibet

When Howie died I
Planned to write down his stories lest I forget
But it's been years and I forgot to
So I think they went with him

Since then
Times have changed
and I
Pay for meaning now
Like
When she kissed me and dissolved on my tongue
Slowly
Before the purple hue engulfed us

I say, she say
and cut at validity
Negating as
Zero does to Infinity
Things like
"Tripping on small things
Keeps you
Looking down"
and

"How many times
Can the floors be scrubbed
Before we admit madness?"

(fire burn bright
if only for one night
kindle it desperately
as it burns out in time)
Five hours of sleep later
Peeling up like a scab
Vying for new flesh

Then later
Miss,
Do you know the pleasure of a cold beer
in the shower?
Riding your tongue
Hot water descending
down your body

Then later
Thinking thinking thinking
"How many pints could it take
To find Past's feeling?
It's got to be at the bottom of one of these."

Then later

Then later

Then later

Then later

Then gone

Originally published in *Iceberg's Poetry* on Medium

Faded Building

I stare at the bottom of the building hanging loftily from my zenith.
A grid pattern forces its will onto me
The dirty of years' wind sticks like a curse
(I suspect it will remain untampered until the end of time.
To my right lays the northern horizon
She is beautiful today
There is a glow at the edge, just above the treeline
And the cloudless blue stands proudly, reaching toward heaven.
Planted to my left and to my south is the leg of the monolith
A small, faded mural of an octopus is placed like a tattoo
The sound of motorized ventilation fills the courtyard with a cutting hum.
I put my smile back on and then I put my best foot back on and then I put it forward and then I scan my card to go back inside.
I won't be going north today.

Originally published in *The Crooked Circle* on Medium

Birds in my shower steam mirror

Birds in my shower steam mirror
And how did you get here, little ones?
Sitting on stems at various heights
Dipping low and soaring the sky, my torso
You will die and I won't know your secrets
Pretty
apt for
a
Reflection

Originally published on Medium

Suburban Night in Late Summer

Treelines the wires' exterior
Human habitat
Human nature
Nature

Dog's bark bouncing
on and off of houses
Rousing the
dog barks
bouncing off the houses
and the tree line
along wires' exterior
Extant in bulbous air
to the deluge of the 347's nighttime precipice of trafficked cars

Cricket chirp cacophony
Swelling auditorium
breaks
Like first snowflake's sky
Prophesizing a Come
along the
treelines
which are
exterior
to the wires

Lamp light hums
front lawn's empty breeze
Central air thumps
the winding-downers in the
reverberating houses
in the human nature
which is nature
interior to the

treeline,
exteriorating the wires

Originally published in *Iceberg's Poetry* on Medium

When You're Nobody

Nobody particularly checks in anymore
Only when
They need
Something
I guess this is the freedom allotted to me
Like that time they ate the apple.
I sure hope it was
good

Nobody particularly
Cares
We're just
Doing it all and looking pleased to make others
Not worry.
I guess that's the freedom allotted to us

Nobody can write love how it actually feels
Unless
That's how it actually feels
Well… then.
I guess that's the freedom allotted to me

Nobody really cleans a constant mess
Searching for pride in infinite rubble
With fluorescent, sterile lights
Overkill, I think
Like the sound of fans
Fast fashion
And car inspections.

We're all grown up with nowhere to go
[Often unapproachable
Sky dimming
I was no-coached

By the ocean I looked out then
Saw waves like homemade icing
Sweetness in the sound and smell
I looked out then
Saw an escape
Plunging deep into the cold
Of early Spring
Raging against
A fickle, tender existence
And I
K**no**w
I didn't do it
And I think I'm glad that I didn't
That is the freedom allotted to us]
We're all grown up with no guide to grow

Originally published on Medium

Acknowledgments

Back in 2019, I began writing poetry because I had to. Inspired by Bukowski and cummings, I started throwing words into the wind on a platform called Medium. I expected very little from it.

Eventually, by fate or by chance (if they are not one and the same), I was noticed by a few people. One became a steady source of support and, over time, a mentor. Through our concordance, he guided me toward a stronger sense of presentation and discipline—lessons that would bring greater recognition.

We both went on to establish close-knit publications on the platform, but that man, has always had a particular gift for kindling community and drawing the best out of poets. His name is Thomas James. He is blunt. He harbors a well-known disdain for New York (having transplanted to Colorado years ago... traitor!). And he can kill you with quotes. More than that, though, he is a friend, a great inspiration, and a modern *fautor artium.*

It is thanks to him that this book has come to fruition. Thomas—thank you for seeing potential in me, and for what you have contributed to modern poetry and its smaller artists.

I would also like to extend my gratitude to the other writers I have met along the way who have offered support and community. We need one another. Ideas and creations are meant for other minds.

Finally, it is those in my personal life—those I hold closest—who have truly made this book possible. They are my wellspring. I will reserve the right to keep that world protected, to maintain a measure of anonymity, but you know who you are, and I love you infinitely. With that, thank you for taking the time to read this. I hope something within these pages resonated with you.

Until next time.

—*Wolf*

www.ingramcontent.com/pod-product-compliance
Lightning Source LLC
LaVergne TN
LVHW010941110826
845149LV00013B/2697

* 9 7 9 8 9 9 9 5 5 5 2 7 4 *